Adam C Miller Present

Facebook Wealth F

Latest Edition: January, 2015

High Quality - Only For Serious Readers

Easy **$500 A Day**
Without having any website or a product!
(Using Clickbank)

DISCLAIMER

The information presented herein represents the views of the author as of the date of publication. Because of the rate with which conditions change, the author reserves the rights to alter and update his opinions based on the new conditions. This manual is for informational purposes only and the author does not accept any responsibilities for any liabilities resulting from the use of this information. While every attempt has been made to verify the information provided here, the author and his referrals cannot assume any responsibility for errors, inaccuracies or omissions. Any slights of people or organizations are unintentional.

This publication is not intended for use as any source of advice such as legal, medical, or accounting. The publisher wants to stress that the information contained herein may be subject to varying international, federal, state, and/or local laws or regulations. The purchaser or reader of this publication assumes responsibility for the use of these materials and information. Adherence to all applicable laws and regulations, including international, federal, state and local governing professional licensing, business practices, advertising, and all other aspects of doing business in the EU, US, Canada or any other jurisdiction is the sole responsibility of the purchaser or reader. Neither the author nor the publisher assume any responsibility or liability whatsoever on the behalf of the purchaser or reader of these materials. Any perceived slight of any individual or organization is purely unintentional.

This book is for personal use only. It should serve as a reference only with no guarantee to any personal or financial gains. Results from usage of materials described in this book may vary. By reading this material, you agree that the author is not liable on any consequences arising from usage of this book.

Important Information From The Author

Hey Guys, to make sure that the method is working perfectly, I checked the authenticity of this method today (i.e. on 2nd January 2015), I followed this method in a step by step manner to verify it and I found it working perfectly & flawlessly. I applied it on a totally new Facebook account which I made today. I added friends using the strategy mentioned in this PDF and within 6 hours I started making money. Latest screenshots (as on 2nd January 2015) of my Facebook account and income proof have been taken and inserted by me in this PDF to give you latest perspective and analysis.

Facebook makes only minor changes in designs and styles after every 6 months, so you should not worry about the changes which Facebook makes. You should apply this method without any hesitation and if you follow it in step by step manner, then I am sure that you'll start making $60-$100 a day in just 3 days and you'll start making $500 a day within just 4 weeks and it's my personal guarantee!

-Adam C Miller
admin@highspeedbusiness.net

Your Rights!

You've Spent **$97.00** To Secure Your Copy Of This Method, So I Want To Give You The Full Value Of Your Money. I Am Offering You The Following Rights On This PDF.

<u>You've Right To:</u>

✓ Share it on Facebook

✓ Sell this report at any price.

✓ Give it away to your subscribers.

✓ Distribute it free of cost.

✓ Share it on forums to earn reputation

✓ Offer as a bonus.

✓ Distribute it like your own product.

✓ Upload and share it on file sharing websites.

Please Note, You <u>Don't</u> Have Any Right To Edit This Report.

Hello friends, my name is Adam C Miller and I am from USA. I am a reputed member on many internet marketing forums & websites. Today, thousands of people on the internet know me for publishing the most realistic internet marketing e-books & reports. Every week, a lot of new people on the internet become my students, learn internet marketing from me and start making money successfully. If you face any difficulty in implementing this method, or if you've any doubt regarding this method then contact me at: admin@highspeedbusiness.net

I never hurry while publishing an e-book. I do research, find new methods & apply them and if I am successful, I tell others about those methods in my e-books. I write an e-book once in 6 months, but it's always the best one. For your information, I will keep publishing newer versions of 'Facebook Wealth Formula' and you can get them into your inbox automatically, if you subscribe to my newsletter. If you have any doubts regarding this method or you face any difficulty, please email me at admin@highspeedbusiness.net

The amount i.e. $97.00 which you've invested in 'Facebook Wealth Formula' is going to be your best investment in internet marketing. I am sure that you'll learn awesome stuff out of this e-book. If you are reading this e-book online then I suggest you to download the e-book on your computer and then start reading it. Reading online won't give you better understanding and hyperlinks in the e-book won't work too. So, it's better to download before you start reading.

If you want to see how many people are making money using Facebook Wealth Formula, then please visit this page. If you want to ask a question regarding this method, please visit here. It will give you immense information & support for using this method.

Thanks
Adam C Miller

Ok! Let's Start...

You might have read many e-books on making money, but no e-book gives you any guarantee that you'll make money, right? But, here is the most realistic and practical e-book you have ever read in your life. It's a complete blueprint of making rock solid income consistently! This is the exact method which I use to make **$500 a day** from my own Facebook account! Using this method, like hundreds of other users of this method, you can reach at **$500 a day in just 4 weeks**, starting from scratch!

First of all you must understand that the success of this method depends upon your Facebook account and the number of friends you've. So, we must create a new Facebook account and add friends. I've explained it in a really simple step by step manner and you should follow it exactly, if you're really interested in making $500/day from your Facebook account.

Step 1: Visit www.facebook.com and create a new Facebook account. If you already have a Facebook account, do NOT use it. Just create a new Facebook account, because in your existing (old) account, your friends are your personal friends and also they're not very niche targeted. Your new Facebook account should look like a profile of 18-20 years old girl. Girls get more attention and gain friends quickly. Name should be sweet & common one. It shouldn't look like a fake profile. It should be sober, natural and simple. Go to www.images.google.com and find the pictures that represent girls like flowers, candles, lips, cleavage (*sorry girls*) etc. and upload one of them as your profile picture. Don't place picture of someone other. Enter as much information as you can into your profile because people don't like empty profiles. *Simple!*

Step 2: After you've created a new Facebook Account, it's the time to add friends to it. You can add maximum 5000 friends to your Facebook account. Your motive should be to exploit this opportunity. This is the most important task. How much money you'll make depends upon the number of friends you have. I'll show you how I added **5000 friends in 7 days only** but you will NEVER need to add 5000 friends to make money. You can start making money as soon as you've only 1000 friends (Just 2 days task).

Step 3: If you start adding friends manually, you can't add 1000 friends even in a year so we'll adopt a trick to add friends really fast! You need to find a good email list generator. Please note, we're talking about an email list generator and NOT about an email extractor. An email extractor which is also known as email scraper or email harvester is totally different from an email list

Facebook Wealth Formula – January, 2015 Edition

generator. Don't ever use email extractor, harvester or scraper because you're going to waste your time because an email extractor will simply harvest email addresses from the internet and give you the list of collected email addresses. There are so many problems in using an email extractor, harvester or scraper. First, an email extractor extracts & collects email addresses from the websites randomly so the number of email addresses is limited upto the email addresses available on the websites i.e just 100, 500 or 1000 email addresses. Second, it will also collect email addresses from the websites of business firms, companies, lawyers and doctors etc. which are of NO USE to you. Definitely, you won't like to send a friend request to a doctor, lawyer, advocate, carpenter or an accounting firm. It can put you in a serious problem. So, don't even think about collecting email addresses from the internet and using them to send friend requests. Makes sense? To give you a clear picture (so that you don't get confused), I've designed this small image.

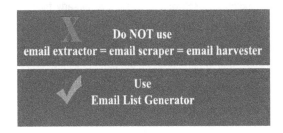

An *email lists generator* is more powerful than an *email extractor*. An *email lists generator* generates lists of supposed email addresses using common names of the people of the countries you want to target. These email addresses belong to the general public and not to the companies, firms or business houses. The best thing is that you can use different combinations of the names, keywords, domain names and random numbers to generate the lists of hundreds of thousands of unique email addresses. Using an *email lists generator* you can target any market you want. For example, you can generate lists of email addresses of those people who're interested in making money, losing weight, poker, credit cards, music, websites, SEO, Twitter or Facebook applications etc. Not only this, you can also target any country you want e.g. USA, UK, Canada, Spain, Nigeria, Australia and all other countries. I downloaded and tested different email lists generators, one after another. It took me 2 weeks and I wasted around $1325 to find the right tool.

Yes, after wasting $1325 and testing different softwares, I found "Acute Email IDs Production Engine". I found it really good because there are two main reasons behind that. First, it's the cheapest in price amongst all the tools I tested and second, it's easy to use & very effective. The best feature is that it saves email addresses lists in the text files which is a very important requirement for our method. It's really cheap in price and you can easily afford it. You can buy it directly from this website, the download is instant. I must say that this is the most important thing which you must have if you want to start making $500/day.

I know I am taking risk by openly recommending a product. You might be thinking that I want to sell you this software, right? **Wrong!** This is not a crappy e-book which contains affiliate links from Clickbank or Commission Junction websites to make sales and earn commission. I am already making **$500 a day**, so few $$ from affiliate commission won't change my life. I am recommending this software because I've already tried many other softwares available online and have wasted a lot of money and time. I don't want you to waste your time and money like I did in searching for the right tool. Although, I've made a recommendation but you're still free to use any tool of your choice but if you're going to buy a software other than Acute Email IDs Production Engine, then please make sure it has following features:

- option to generate unlimited email addresses lists
- target any country you want
- target any niche you want
- add random numbers while generating emails
- save email lists in text file (.txt)

While using this software I found that more than 80% of generated email addresses really exist and it's really good. Means, if you generate a list of 4000 email addresses, to send friend requests to, then 3200 will be real ones and this is a fantastic figure. You don't need to send emails to these people. Facebook has a special feature to perform this function.

Step 4: Using your email lists generator, generate an email addresses list and save it in a text file. It should not take more than 60 seconds. Acute Email IDs Production Engine automatically saves email addresses in the text files (.txt). If you're going to choose a different email lists generator then make sure that it has this feature because it's very important.

Step 5: Now, Facebook won't allow you to directly upload this text file containing email addresses list. You need to put this email addresses list in a special format to upload on Facebook. Click here to download *'contacts.csv'* file on your computer which is already in that format which Facebook accepts. After downloading, open this file in MS_Excel. In case you don't have MS_Excel then you can install "OpenOffice" on your computer by downloading it from here, it's free! If you're using "OpenOffice", then right click on *'contacts.csv'* file icon and choose **Open With > OpenOffice.org Calc** like shown below:

On next window, it will ask how you would like to open this file. Make the following settings. Please note that the option 'Comma' should be checked and the option 'Space' should be unchecked. After doing these settings, click OK and file will open.

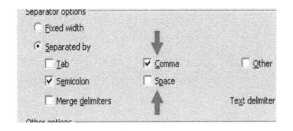

After opening, this file will look like as below. This is an empty file, because it's just a format which Facebook accepts.

	A	B	C	D	E	F
1	Name	E-mail Add	Home Stre	Home City	Home Pos	Home Stat
2						
3						
4						
5						

Step 6: Now, open your **Text File** in which email addresses list (you just generated) was saved. Copy all email addresses from it, come back to 'contacts.csv' file, right click and paste all email addresses under the column '**E-mail Addresses**' as shown in the picture below. Leave all other columns blank.

	A	B	C	D
1	Name	E-mail Add	Home Stre	Home City	H
2				
3			✂ Cut	
4			📋 Copy	
5			📋 Paste	
6				
7			Paste Special...	
8			Insert...	
9				

After pasting email addresses, 'contacts.csv' file will look like as below:

	A	B	C	D	E
1	Name	E-mail Add	Home Stre	Home City	Home Pos	H
2		████	tinternet.com			
3		████	rizon.net			
4		████	mail.com			
5		████	agift.com			
6		████	oo.com			
7		████	gmail.com			
8		████	@yahoo.com			
9		████	ol.com			
10		████	aol.com			
11		████	hoo.com			
12		████	@hotmail.com			
13		████	eji@gmail.com			
14		████	ja@gmail.com			

Step 7: When you save this file, MS_Excel (or OpenOffice) will ask you a new file name but you can simply overwrite the file choosing the same name. Choose 'Yes' if you see the following screen:

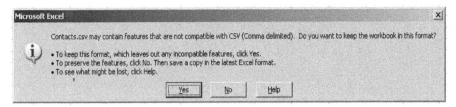

Trust me, you've done 60% work and are very close to **$500 a day**. Was it difficult? I don't think so! If you think it was difficult, then simply read it again and apply these steps while you're reading. You may find this process a bit boring, but remember **$500 a day** is not a small amount.

Here's the recap of what we've done so far:

1. Create a new <u>Facebook</u> account. Your profile should look like a profile of 18-20 years old girl. It should look simple, sober, natural and real.
2. Generate an email list using an email list generator of your choice. I used <u>Acute Email IDs Production Engine</u>. Do NOT use any email extractor, harvester or a scraper.
3. Download and install "OpenOffice" <u>from here</u>. (No need if you already have MS_Excel).
4. Download 'contacts.csv' file <u>from here</u>. Copy email addresses from text file and paste them in 'contacts.csv' file and save it.

Is it clear? Let's go further...

Step 8: Now, we'll upload 'contacts.csv' file on Facebook so that Facebook can send friend requests to these people. If they're on Facebook, then they'll get friend request instantly and as soon as they accept your friend request, they'll become your friends. In case they're not on Facebook, then Facebook will send them invitation to join Facebook to become your friends. In both situations, you win. This step is really simple! Login to your Facebook account, visit this page: <u>http://www.facebook.com/invite.php</u> and click 'Import your email addresses' option.

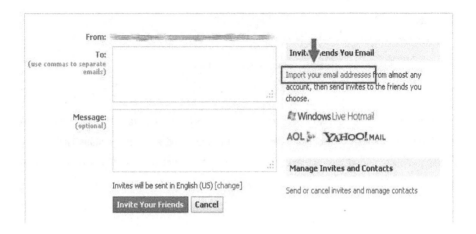

Step 9: Now Facebook is asking from where you want to import email addresses (source). Click on the option 'Other Tools' as shown below:

<u>Special Note:</u>

Facebook keeps playing with its options and sometimes you may not be able to find 'Other Tools' as an option. In that case simply click 'other services' or find if there is an option like 'Outlook Express' etc.

Step 10: Thereafter, Click "Choose File" button and simply browse 'contacts.csv' file (in which you pasted email addresses and saved) and then click 'Upload Contacts' button.

Step 11: As soon as the file is uploaded, Facebook will show you the list of your contacts it found in that file. Click 'Select All' checkbox and click 'Add to invite' button.

Invite Your Friends

Choose how you communicate with friends. See how it works or manage imported contacts.

Invite Friends and Family to Facebook

☑ Select All/None ⬅ ①

☑
☑
☑
☑
☑
☑
☑
☑
☑

② ➡ Add to Invite   Cancel

Step 12: You'll see that Facebook has added all the friends in the invitation list. Now click 'Invite Your Friends' button and that's it! Facebook will send invitation to all these people. If the people on invitation list are already on Facebook then they'll get friend request on your behalf and if they're not on Facebook, then they'll get an invitation to join Facebook to become your friends.

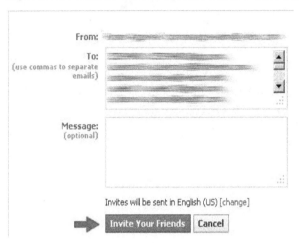

Step 13: After sending invitations, open 'contacts.csv' file again and delete all email addresses from it. To invite more people, simply generate a fresh list of email addresses using 'Acute Email IDs Production Engine' and paste it in 'contacts.csv' file and save the file again. Now, upload this file again on Facebook by repeating the same process to invite more people. You can do it as many times as you want by generating fresh email addresses every time.

On first day, I sent **invitations to 800 people** and it took **just 20 minutes!**

Didn't you find it easy?

Yes! It's a very easy process, if you don't understand it then apply this process while reading this e-book, it will make things a lot easier. Follow this practice only two times a day. It takes only 2 minutes to generate hundreds of email addresses.

Ok, when I sent invitation to 800 friends on first day, 334 people were already on Facebook and they got friend requests immediately and the remaining 466 people who were not on Facebook got invitation to join Facebook via email.

...Result?

I added **26 friends in 1 hour** only.

You know, Facebook activities go viral. When you add a friend, it's displayed on walls of both of you and a lot of other people notice your profile and they also like to add you as a friend. Your work is just to accept these invitations.

See, how many friend requests I got within next 2 hours.

Yes, there were **39 friend requests** and my job was just to add them one by one.

Here is the screenshot of huge number of friend requests, I got on the same day, I sent the invitations. As soon as you get friend requests, you can add them as your friends by clicking 'Confirm' button. I've blurred the names of Facebook users to protect their privacy, as per Facebook "Terms of use".

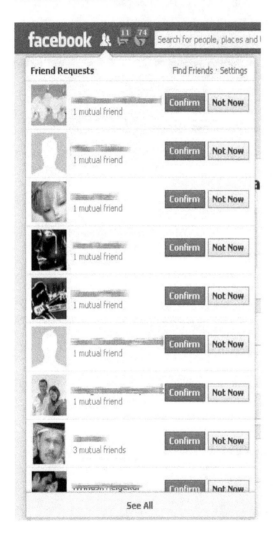

I added all of them as friends and now I had **63 friends**. **(All in just 3 hours)**

After around **8 hours**, I checked again and got amazed that there were **more than 250 friends** in my Facebook account. **That was a fantastic figure!** Most of the people to whom I sent friend requests had added me (just because of 'hot' girl profile.) Means, I got more than **250 Facebook friends in just one day**! That was more than enough for me.

On **2nd Day**, I generated more email addresses using 'Acute Email IDs Production Engine' pasted them in 'contacts.csv' file and uploaded it on Facebook and invited more people. This time I invited around 3000 people. Again, those who were already on Facebook got friend requests on my behalf and those who were not on Facebook got invitations via email. At an average, generating email lists and uploading 'contacts.csv' file was taking only few minutes. I was doing this process just 2 times a day so I was spending only 20-25 minutes daily for this work.

On late evening of **2ⁿᵈ Day**, I checked my profile and found that I had **more than 600 friends.**

I was taking screenshots every day, because, I was an active member at Digitalpoint Forum and was sharing my progress in this thread. The forum members were so excited with the results that they started sharing their Facebook accounts urls and their personal email addresses to add even more friends, faster. It was against Facebook as well as Digitalpoint rules so forum moderators had to delete the thread.

Anyhow, now I was getting 70-90 friend requests daily and was adding a lot of friends every day. I was uploading 'contacts.csv' file daily to my Facebook account by generating fresh email addresses lists using my email lists generator.

I took this screenshot on **3ʳᵈ Day**. Look at the huge jump in the number of friends.

Day - 3

Actually, Facebook doesn't allow you to send 20 or more friend requests manually but, when you invite them with this method, this limit doesn't apply.

These were **some of the daily pictures** of Recent Activity on my Facebook timeline:

On **5th Day**, I had more than **2200 friends**.

Day-6 - Ultimate Growth Day!

This was the 7th Day & I achieved the target of adding 5000 friends.

Still, there were <u>a lot of pending friend requests</u> and when I tried to add them as friends I got this message from Facebook:

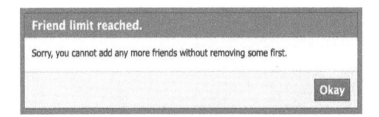

Like I already mentioned that the maximum number of friends which you can add is 5000 only but **you don't need to add 5000 friends and you can start making money <u>as soon as you've 1000 friends</u>**. So after I reached this number of friends, people couldn't send me friend requests anymore. If someone would send me a friend request he'll see the following error message:

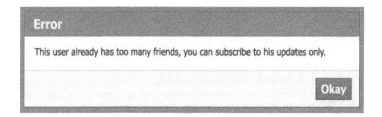

Once you reach at this level, your **<u>80% work</u>** is complete! I added 5000 friends in just 7 days, but you need only 1000 friends to make money so it can be completed only in 2 days ;)

Here is a **quick** summary of what we did to add 5000 friends in 7 days only:

1. Visit www.facebook.com and create a new Facebook account.
2. Get a good email lists generator and generate an email list, it would be saved in a text file automatically if you're using Acute Email IDs Production Engine. If you're using another email lists generator then make sure it has the option to generate unlimited email lists and save them in text file.
3. Click here to download a readymade file format to upload on Facebook, the name of the file is 'contacts.csv'. Facebook won't accept any format other than this one.
4. Open 'contacts.csv' in MS_Excel. If you don't have MS_Excel then you can download open office and install it on your computer. Thereafter, right click on 'contacts.csv' file icon and choose open with > *openoffice.org calc*
5. Copy email addresses from text file saved by email list generator and paste them into 'contacts.csv' under the heading 'E-mail Addresses'. Leave other columns blank and save it.
6. Goto http://www.facebook.com/invite.php page and click 'Import your email addresses' option and then choose 'Other Tools'.
7. Browse and upload 'contacts.csv' file there. After file is uploaded it will show all the contacts.
8. Click 'Select All' and then 'Add to Invite' button and then click 'Invite your friends'.

Step 16: Creating a Facebook Page:

In order to make money from your Facebook account you must have a Facebook page. **As soon as you've just 1000 friends**, you can create a Facebook page and start making money from the same day. That means, if you start today, you can start making money within 4 days. (Adding 1000 friends takes 3 days only and you can create a Facebook page and start making money from 4th day). Although, it will be $50 - $70/day in the beginning and within 4 weeks you'll reach at $500/day. But even $50/day in just 4 days is a BIG achievement! *Isn't it?*

It's all <u>WITHOUT</u> investment!

Let's understand this way

If you start on	You'll have 1000 friends on	You can create your Facebook page and <u>start making atleast $50/day</u> from
Monday	Wednesday	Thursday
Tuesday	Thursday	Friday
Wednesday	Friday	Saturday
Thursday	Saturday	Sunday
Friday	Sunday	Monday
Saturday	Monday	Tuesday
Sunday	Tuesday	Wednesday

You can create a Facebook page for anything you want. It may be about a particular subject you like for example a celebrity, computers, mobiles, laptops, games, dating sites, matrimonial, weight loss, health tips or anything. All you need is a Facebook account and if you've a Facebook account with 1000 friends, **then *you've gold in your hands!***

After creating a Facebook page, you can start making money from the same day. You'll start selling products and earning commissions from your fan page from **FIRST DAY** and this is my promise. Not only this, as the number of "Likes" for your fan page increases, you'll get even more "Likes" automatically at a rapid speed and you'll make money every day on complete autopilot!

Most Important Lesson - Remember

Before creating a fan page, you must have at least 1000 friends. That doesn't mean that you can't create a fan page without having 1000 friends but if you create a fan page before having 1000 friends, then your page will not get enough exposure and it will be difficult to earn money from it. **Let's move the next step...**

✓ **How To Create A Page That Brings Avalanche Of Money To You!**

First of all, visit http://www.facebook.com/pages/create.php to start creating a page, choose "Cause or Community" as page type and fill in all the possible details into your fan page.

Add an attractive image to your page to gain more attention. If you want to create a picture yourself then you can visit Google Images to get an idea. If you find anything incomplete in your fan page then complete it first before asking your friends to join it. Besides it, your page should have an attractive and meaningful name which is related to the type of product you can easily sell.

For example, if you're interested in selling a product about "weight loss" then the title of your page can be any of the following:

- *Stay fit by losing a bit – Get free weight loss tips every day*
- *Lose weight quickly – free daily diet info*
- *Fast results – Ultimate weight loss tips*

After your page is complete in all respects, it's the time to make money :)

How to start making money without having any website or a product?

Because you don't have a website or a product to sell, so we'll take help of Clickbank. Clickbank.com is a digital marketplace where thousands of products are sold every day. It's one of the most popular website amongst those who want to make money online without any website or a product. It's completely free to join. Clickbank is that website where hundreds of informative products like ebooks, softwares and the membership sites are sold every day.

There're 3 types of people who use Clickbank:

1. **Vendors** – Those who create & sell the products like ebooks, softwares, memberships & courses on Clickbank. They're the sellers actually. Generally, the products sold on Clickbank are downloadable.
2. **Customers** - Those who buy the products from Clickbank website.
3. **Affiliates** – Those who spread the links of these Clickbank products on the internet to let people know about these products. When someone clicks on an affiliate link and buy the product, then affiliates earn commissions. Means, an affiliate is a middleman between customer and vendor (seller) and brings the customers to seller's website.

Note: You're going to work as an affiliate in this system.

Your work is just posting affiliate links of Clickbank products on your Facebook page and sending the customers to seller's website. You'll earn commission as soon as someone buys something after clicking on your link.

Now, I'll tell you how to make $500/day by working as Clickbank "affiliate" and using your Facebook page. You'll get this money transferred to your bank account whenever you want. Your work is just posting the links of Clickbank products on Facebook. When someone clicks on your link and buy any product, you'll earn commission. The commissions on the products are really high and ranges from **50% - 85%** of price of the product. That means, if you post a link to a $50 product and commission is 60% then **you'll get $30 for just ONE SALE!**

You won't have to do anything as your work is just bringing the customers to the product website, that's it! As soon as a sale is completed through your link, the commission will be credited to your account and you can withdraw it whenever you want. Clickbank pays commissions via bank cheque or direct bank transfer. You can choose the option in your account. But you can enter your bank account details in your Clickbank account only after you've earned $100 in commission.

Creating a Clickbank account: So just visit at www.clickbank.com and create a free account. Fill in all the required details in your account to complete it in all respects.

Another Important Lesson

In case you don't find your country name in the signup form on Clickbank, then don't worry. For example, if you're from Nigeria then you'll not find "Nigeria" as an option in the list of countries, but still you can create account on Clickbank and earn commissions. While signing up on Clickbank, enter any fake address and choose any country like USA. After you've earned $100 in your Clickbank account, you can enter your bank account details there and money will be transferred to your bank account and it doesn't matter in which country you're located. They'll ask you just your Bank Name, Bank Account Number and IFSC Code (Mentioned on your bank cheque book) and you'll start receiving money in your bank account **even if** you're in that country which is not in Clickbank's list. Now, please don't share this tip with anyone. ☺

Step 15: **Generating your affiliate link:**

After logging into your Clickbank account you can start making money instantly. Simply visit this link: https://accounts.clickbank.com/account/marketplace.htm This is the marketplace of the Clickbank where you can see all the products being sold on Clickbank. At this page, you'll see an option to find the products:

Enter any keyword to find the products according to your taste. For example, if you can sell products related to "Weight Loss" then enter "weight loss" as your keyword and if your interest is in "Forex" then enter "Forex" to find the products. After entering the keyword, you'll get a list of lot of products. There's a button saying "Promote" in front of each of the product like shown below. Click on the "Promote" button in front of that product which you choose to promote. You must **read this article** which tells how to choose the best products to promote. But don't make it so hard, just choose any product whose price, commissions and the website appeals you.

When you click "Promote", a popup window will appear. In the popup window, enter your Clickbank Nickname and click "Create" to generate the affiliate link of that product. **Nickname is generally the username of your Clickbank account** and is automatically entered while generating affiliate link.

Account Nickname: james980

Tracking ID (Optional):

Create

In the next window the HopLink (affiliate link) will appear in the first field and HTML code in the second field. Copy the HopLink URL from the first field. You do **NOT** need the HTML code. That's it!

"Hoplink" or "affiliate link" is the same thing

Affiliate Program: HopLink for 'VENDOR'   Close

English ▼

ClickBank pays you 75.0% when you sell [   ]'s product. To refer a customer send them to this domain name:

http://xxxxxxxxxxxxxxxxxxxxxxxxxxxxxxxxx.hop.clickbank.net/ ◄════

Copy the following HopLink HTML code and add it to your web page:

<a href="http://xxxxxxxxxxxxxxxxxxxxxxxxxxxxx.hop.clickbank.net/" target="_top">Click Here!</a>

Congratulations! Now you've your own affiliate link or hoplink. This hoplink has a Tracking ID linked to your Clickbank account. Now when a visitor clicks on your hoplink, he'll be redirected to the website of that product which you selected to promote and if the visitor makes a purchase, you'll earn commission.

Testing your hoplink (affiliate link): It's important to check your hoplink (or affiliate link), before you proceed further. To test, if your Hoplink (or affiliate link) is working accurately or not, paste the HopLink into internet browser (internet explorer, chrome, firefox etc.) address bar and hit Enter. The HopLink will take you to the product website. Read the sales page and, just for testing purpose, click something like "Purchase Now/Buy Now/Download Now" etc. on that page, just like you are a buyer. You'll see the order form page. Scroll down to the bottom of the order page like shown in the image below.

1. If your affiliate link is working properly, you should see: [affiliate = yournickname]
2. If your affiliate link is not working properly, you will see: [affiliate = none]

Below shown picture shows a working affiliate link in which username of a Clicbank affiliate is showing up.

Go to mobile orderform

Copyright © 2011 Click Sales Inc. ClickBank / 917 Lusk St / Suite 200 / Boise ID 83706.

Secure Payments

[affiliate = james980]

Now, you've your hoplink ready and we need people who click on your link and buy the product. Remember, the more clicks you get, the more sales will be there and more commissions you'll earn. Never post any HopLink on your Facebook wall otherwise you'll be blocked by Facebook and your account will be deleted. You can post Clickbank HopLinks only on a Facebook page created by you.

<u>Now, let's start earning money with your first post</u>

You already have a Facebook page, now it's the time to post status update and tell your friends about it. Status update is anything that you share with your fans on your page. I promote "Weight Loss" products. Every day, I post a free tip on losing weight + affiliate link (hoplink) as a status update. I find new tips every day from the internet and post them on my page with my Clickbank affiliate link. Here's an example of an ideal status update:

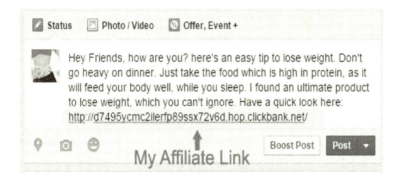

After posting a status update, click "Build Audience" button on your page and then click on "Invite Friends" option.

It will open a widget "Invite Friends" on your fan page. In that widget Facebook shows all of your friends and there's a button "Invite" in front of the name of every friend.

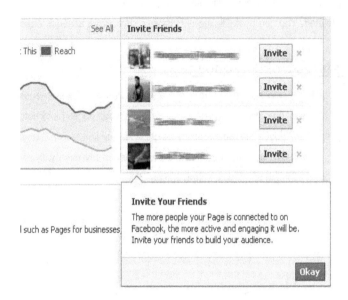

Once you click "Invite" button in front of your friend name, Facebook will send invitation to your friend to join your fan page. Unfortunately, Facebook doesn't allow inviting all the friends in one go. So, you can invite them only <u>one by one</u> and it makes it a time consuming task. But remember, once you've invited all of your friends, you're going to see a lot of clicks on your affiliate link and you'll earn a lot of commissions in a really short period of time. If you can't finish inviting all the friends in one day or in one sitting then no problem! You can invite the remaining friends on another day and so on. Remember, the more friends you invite the more money you'll be making so don't be lazy in inviting the friends. Once someone "Likes" your page, he starts getting updates about your fan page on his wall, automatically. Means, your fans will get notification every time you post something on your page.

✓ How to make your fan page go viral!

Tip 1: Keep posting newer things on your wall about your fan page. Ask people to join your fan page to get free tips in your niche. Repeat this process few times a day and you will be amazed on seeing the tremendous growth.

Tip 2: Use 'Discussion' tab on your page to start discussions on your topic like 'weight loss' in my case. People like conversations and sharing ideas. Give them some tips and they will share their tips too. This is really simple, just like chatting on your Yahoo messenger or any other discussion forum. You'll also have administrative rights of your fan page, so enjoy it!

MAY I TELL YOU AGAIN?

Like I said earlier that you can start making money from 4th Day because in 2 days you can add 1000 friends. On 3rd Day, you can create a fan page and post something with your affiliate link and on 4th Day, you can invite your friends to your fan page. As they'll read your post and like to know more, they'll definitely click on your affiliate link and will buy something from the website you're promoting.

As soon as I had 1000 friends, I started inviting friends to my fan page. It took me 7 days to add 5000 friends but on the other hand, I was also inviting my FB friends to my page. I finished inviting 5000 friends in 10 days, but you can do this task in just 1 day, because you can start inviting them as soon as you've 1000 friends. When I finished inviting all of my 5000 friends on 10th day midnight, I went to the bed feeling tired and sleepy. When I checked my Facebook account on 11th day (next day) noon, I got a big surprise! I saw that **533 users** liked my fan page and it was a huge response.

When one of your friends "Like" your page, it's posted on his wall. Some of his friends may also like to visit your page and "Like" it and then their friends & so on... Your work is just to wait and watch now! So, when on first day, 533 users liked my fan page, it was posted on their walls and you can imagine how much exposure my fan page got on the same day.

Day - 12 - Next day, when I checked the stats, I almost jumped in the air! See the viral growth! It's RAPID!

Day-13 – More than 100% increase in "Likes".

Day-14 (A day of tremendous growth, this is how Facebook works in a viral way)

Day-17

Day-19

Day-22

Day-24

Day-26

Day – 28

On 29th Day, I had <u>more than 50000 Fans</u> – 2nd Target Achieved!!

Photos   Likes

Remember: You must have minimum 1000 friends to share your page otherwise, your page will not be popular. Your first target should be to add atleast 1000 friends to your FB account. This is totally easy and can be achieved in just 48 hours like I showed you. I showed you that 50,000 "Likes" can be gained in just 30 days but you don't need to get 50,000 "Likes" to make money because you will start making money even when you've **just 200 "Likes".**

Remember:: As soon as you've 1000 FB friends and 200 "Likes" you'll start making money.

✓ How many status updates & how much effective they are?

Just 2-3 updates a day will be enough. It shouldn't take more than 25-30 minutes a day. I post health tips, weight loss tips, diet information with my Clickbank affiliate links as status updates. You should also do the same and encourage your fans to click on your link to get more information about the products.

Let's Calculate Your Earning

Now suppose, you are too bad in writing status updates and most of the people ignore your status updates. But just imagine that only 1% of your fans click on your affiliate link and make purchases (this is minimum), then you'll get at least 2 sales a day, and this is just the beginning. With the passage of time, you'll get more friends, more likes and more sales.

200 fans X 1% = 2 sales a day - This is just the beginning
What if you've 50,000 "Likes" like I have?

The figures I showed you are really easy to achieve and we've taken everything at its minimum. For example, getting 1000 FB friends is really easy with the help of a good email list generator like Acute Email IDs Production Engine. Once you've 1000 friends, having 200 "Likes" is too easy and is just a childish game. Having 200 Likes means you can start making money because if only 1% people read and purchase the items from your affiliate links then you'll start getting 2 sales a day.

Let me show you my Clickbank earnings!

I get this money transferred to my bank account regularly

WEEKLY SALES SNAPSHOT

Week Ending	Gross Sales
2015-01-06 (current week)	$4386.75
2014-12-30	$4236.30
2014-12-23	$4028.19
2014-12-16	$2612.66
2014-12-09	$3749.11

DAILY SALES SNAPSHOT

Date		Gross	Trend
Fri	Jan 02	$524.53	
Thu	Jan 01	$554.20	
Wed	Dec 31	$600.36	
Tue	Dec 30	$517.42	
Mon	Dec 29	$521.96	
Sun	Dec 28	$584.74	
Sat	Dec 27	$563.49	
Fri	Dec 26	$520.06	
Thu	Dec 25	$536.76	
Wed	Dec 24	$605.90	
Tue	Dec 23	$503.29	
Mon	Dec 22	$526.66	
Sun	Dec 21	$600.58	
Sat	Dec 20	$556.83	
Fri	Dec 19	$565.22	

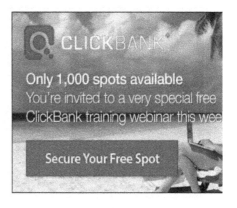

Only 1,000 spots available
You're invited to a very special free
ClickBank training webinar this wee

Secure Your Free Spot

CLICKBANK INSIGHTS

ClickBank Insights provides you with a customized list of vendor rec your customers' buyer behavior. Results are based on data collecte transactions across our entire network of vendors and affiliates.

At this time your account has not registered enough sales to calculat display ClickBank insights.

Visit the Knowledge Base for more information about ClickBank Insig

I remain too busy in my other online businesses and the internet marketing campaigns, so I don't get time to post 2-3 updates daily. I usually post only 3-4 posts in a week and I manage to get around 20 sales a day because I keep getting traffic from previous posts too. I usually promote products which give commission of $20-$30 per sale, so I make $500/day really easy. You'll not believe, but trust me, that to make $500/day I don't have to do anything except posting some updates on my fan page. **This is 100% autopilot!** I feel so safe about my family, life and the future because this is 100% secure and surefire way of making money from your Facebook account without any investment, website or a product. In the beginning, you will have easy 2-3 sales a day which will make you around $50-$60 a day but soon you'll have more friends, more fans and more clicks on your affiliate links. You can reach $500/day in just 4 weeks, like I showed you. *Just imagine, how your life will change if you start making $500/day with just 30 minutes a day.*

Here're some of the other products which will sell easily on Facebook. Because majority of the Facebook users are 20-40 years old, so you can sell anything amongst the following:
- Weight Loss (Hot niche)
- Games, Music and MP3 (Hot niche)
- Acne Treatment (Hot niche)
- Dating offers (Hot niche)
- Pregnancy control
- Teen parenting
- Facebook applications
- Surveys etc.
- Mobile ringtones etc. (Hot niche)

A true short story: Few weeks back, my sister in law asked me to recommend her a good method to make money online and I gave her a copy of Facebook Wealth Formula. She applied it and added **1200** FB fans in just **4 days** and now she is simply offering Clickbank products to her Facebook friends & fans and guess what? She's making more than **$150 a day** in commissions and it's without any website and own product.

There are a lot of opportunities to make money with Facebook. Once you've got around 1000 friends, you can offer them surveys to complete, sell your own product, direct Facebook traffic to your website or blog, you can offer them "Email Submit" offers and much more and you can make a lot of cash with your FB friends. The main thing is adding friends to your account which can be easily done with email list generator. There are a lot of websites who pay you for just bringing visitors and having them fill a simple online form or just submitting their email addresses on the website. **Always remember,** once you've added 1000 friends then there's GOLD in your hands and you just need to monetize that traffic. Your top most task should be to add 1000 friends in your FB account and that can be done in just 2 days. Thereafter you can start making money really simple by just monetizing Facebook traffic.

ATTENTION:

Let me help you further so that you don't fail! – Read Below!

You won't believe but I am going to help you in implementing this method successfully, but for that purpose, you need to email me **within next 30 minutes**. I don't want you to just read this e-book and close it. I want you to become successful in making money with your Facebook account, so, I am going to help you even further. If you're really determined about changing your life, then just email me with the subject line "I am ready to implement FWF". (There is no need to send any email if you don't have any question and you think that can implement this system yourself. You're a genius!!) But if you want to discuss more, then before sending the email, please make sure that you've done **two simple tasks** so that I can be sure that you're really determined about making money and not wasting my time.

Task 1 – Create a new FB account and fill all the necessary information to complete your profile. Your existing FB account will not work and it doesn't matter how many friends you've. Thereafter, create a Clickbank account.

Task 2 – You must have bought a good email list generator like Acute Email IDs Production Engine or any other software which works like Acute.

As soon as you've completed these simple two tasks, send me an email **within 30 minutes** at admin@highspeedbusiness.net with subject line "I am ready to implement FWF" and write anything you want to discuss in email body. (There is no need to send any email if you don't have any question and you think that can implement this system yourself. Bravo!!) Trust me, as soon as I get your email I'll tell you about those Clickbank products which you can promote on your Facebook account and can earn $100 in just 24 hours – my personal guarantee!!

A lot of people after reading "Facebook Wealth Formula" are making <u>more than $100 a day in their first week.</u> Click here to see, how many people all around the world are making money with this Facebook Wealth Formula. I've spent a really long time to develop this perfect system which guarantees that you'll be making <u>$500 a day within 4 weeks</u>. I don't want you to just read and close this e-book. My purpose is not to just "sell" you this guide and earn $97.00. I want to make you successful in making money with this perfect system. If you really want to make money, then just reading this report is not enough, you'll have to "take action". Most of the people don't make any money because they just read, read & read but don't take any action. So, do yourself a favor, don't let this opportunity go, because this opportunity won't come back! Stop thinking and start doing.

TAKE ACTION NOW!
It's "YOUR" Time To Make Money

Click here for a typical action plan

Have a great luck!
Your Friend,

Adam C Miller

TYPICAL ACTION PLAN

Day 1

Start right now and download all the important and necessary items, right away.

A. Create your Facebook account and complete your profile accordingly as mentioned in this e-book earlier.

B. Buy email lists generator, download it and get used to it. Check how email lists generator works and how to generate and save email lists on your computer.

C. Send me an email (admin@highspeedbusiness.net) with subject line "I am ready to implement FWF". No need to send email if you can implement FWF yourself and you don't have any question. You can master it, trust me!

Day 2

Create necessary accounts:

D. Create your Clickbank account (no need if you already have a website and a product to sell). Understand Clickbank marketplace and how affiliate links work.

E. Download 'OpenOffice' and install it on your computer (No need if you already have MS_Excel).

F. Download 'contacts.csv' file from here

Day 3

After you've everything set and ready, start applying this method without any delay. Read all the steps of this e-book again and try to apply them while you're reading.

If you follow this method in the same manner as I've described then I am sure, you'll start making money in just **4 days straight** and it's **my personal guarantee!** In case you've any doubt, contact me at admin@highspeedbusiness.net and you can also subscribe to my newsletter for more high quality stuff, updates and **internet marketing coaching**.

Thanks

Adam C Miller